HTML Essentials & Advanced Concepts

Introduction to HTML

HTML, which stands for HyperText Markup Language, is the standard language used to create and design web pages. Developed in the early 1990s by Tim Berners-Lee, HTML has played a foundational role in the World Wide Web's evolution. Over the years, HTML has gone through several iterations, with each version introducing new features and capabilities to accommodate the changing landscape of web development.

The evolution of HTML started with the initial release of HTML 1.0 in 1993, providing a basic structure for web documents. Subsequent versions, such as HTML 2.0, HTML 3.2, and HTML 4.01, brought improvements in terms of functionality and layout options. However, it was the introduction of HTML5 in 2014 that marked a significant milestone in the history of HTML. HTML5 not only enhanced the language with new elements and attributes but also focused on supporting multimedia and improving the overall user experience.

One of the key reasons for HTML's enduring relevance in web development is its adaptability to the evolving needs of the internet. HTML has consistently embraced new technologies and trends, such as responsive design and mobile optimization, to ensure that web pages can be accessed seamlessly across various devices and platforms. Additionally, HTML's semantic structure has made it easier for search engines to index and understand web content, contributing to improved SEO practices.

In its current version, HTML continues to be the backbone of the web, working in conjunction with CSS for styling and JavaScript for interactivity. The latest specifications, including HTML Living Standard, reflect the collaborative efforts of the web community to refine and standardize the language for modern web development practices.

Understanding HTML Tags and Elements

HTML, the backbone of web development, relies on fundamental building blocks known as tags and elements. Tags are the structural components used to define different parts of a webpage, while elements consist of the opening tag, content, and closing tag, collectively forming the building blocks of HTML documents.

Tags: Tags are enclosed within angle brackets (< >) and are used to define the structure of an HTML document. They are essential for indicating how content should be displayed on a webpage. Tags are often paired as opening and closing tags to encapsulate content. Opening tags denote the beginning of an element, while closing tags signify the end. For example, the opening tag <html> indicates the start of an HTML document, while the closing tag </html> marks its end.

Elements: Elements comprise the entire content enclosed between the opening and closing tags. They consist of the tag name, attributes (optional), and the content. For instance, the <head> element contains meta-information about the document, the <body> element encapsulates the visible content of the webpage, the <title> element specifies the title of the document displayed in the browser tab, and the <p> element defines paragraphs of text.

Examples of Common HTML Tags:

1. <html>: Defines the root of an HTML document.
2. <head>: Contains metadata and links to external resources.
3. <body>: Encloses the main content of the webpage.
4. <title>: Specifies the title of the webpage displayed in the browser.
5. <p>: Represents a paragraph of text on the webpage.

Understanding these basic components of HTML is crucial for structuring content effectively and creating well-formed web pages. By mastering the usage of tags and elements, developers can craft visually appealing and semantically meaningful websites that cater to modern web standards.

Working with Texts and Links

In HTML, managing text formatting is essential for creating visually appealing and structured web pages. HTML offers various tags to format text and create a well-organized content layout. Here are some commonly used text formatting tags in HTML:

Heading Tags

Heading tags, ranging from <h1> to <h6>, are used to define headings and subheadings on a webpage. The <h1> tag represents the main heading, while <h2> to <h6> are used for subheadings with decreasing levels of importance.

Paragraph Tag

The <p> tag is utilized to create paragraphs of text on a webpage. It is crucial for organizing content into readable blocks and separating different sections of text effectively.

Bold, Italic, and Underline Tags

- <b> tag: This tag is used to make text bold, highlighting important information.
- <i> tag: Italicizes text, providing emphasis or differentiation for certain words or phrases.
- <u> tag: Underlines text, typically used to indicate hyperlinks but can also be applied for other formatting purposes.

Creating Hyperlinks

Hyperlinks play a vital role in connecting web pages and enhancing user navigation. In HTML, hyperlinks are created using the <a> tag, with the href attribute specifying the URL destination when the link is clicked. Additionally, the title attribute allows for providing a tooltip when hovering over the link, enhancing user experience. The target attribute defines how the linked page should open, whether in the same tab or a new window.

By utilizing these text formatting tags and hyperlink attributes effectively, web developers can structure content, emphasize key information, and provide seamless navigation for users browsing the web pages.

Embedding Images and Other Media in HTML

When it comes to enhancing the visual appeal and interactivity of a webpage, embedding images and other media elements is a fundamental aspect of web development. HTML provides specific tags to facilitate the seamless integration of multimedia content, including images, videos, and audio files. Let's delve into the process of embedding these elements using HTML tags and attributes.

Embedding Images with <img> Tag

The <img> tag is the primary element used to insert images into an HTML document. To display an image, the src attribute within the <img> tag specifies the image file's location or URL. By setting the src attribute to the appropriate image source, web developers can ensure that the image is rendered correctly on the webpage. Additionally, the alt attribute is used to provide alternative text for the image, which serves as a textual description in case the image fails to load or for accessibility purposes.

Adjusting Image Dimensions

To control the size of the displayed image, developers can adjust the image dimensions using the width and height attributes within the <img> tag. By specifying the desired width and height values in pixels, percentages, or other units, developers can ensure that the image is displayed at the intended size without distortion or stretching.

Embedding Video and Audio Content

In addition to images, HTML supports the embedding of video and audio content using the <video> and <audio> tags, respectively. These tags allow developers to include multimedia elements directly within the webpage, providing users with a richer and more engaging browsing experience. Similar to the <img> tag, the <video> and <audio> tags can be customized with various attributes to control playback, volume, and display options.

By leveraging these HTML tags for embedding images, videos, and audio files, web developers can create dynamic and multimedia-rich web pages that captivate and inform users effectively. The ability to seamlessly integrate visual and auditory content enhances the overall user experience and enables developers to craft compelling websites that cater to diverse audience preferences.

Building and Styling Forms

Creating HTML forms for user input involves utilizing the <form> tag to structure the form elements effectively. These elements can include text fields, radio buttons, checkboxes, dropdown menus, and more, allowing users to interact with the webpage by submitting data. Understanding how to design and implement forms is crucial for collecting information from users and enhancing the interactivity of web pages.

Using the <form> Tag

The <form> tag serves as the container for all form elements and defines the boundary of the form on the webpage. This tag encapsulates input fields, buttons, and other form components, specifying where the user input will be collected and processed. By setting attributes such as action and method within the <form> tag, developers can determine the destination URL for form submission and the HTTP method to be used (e.g., GET or POST).

Input Fields and Form Controls

Text fields, checkboxes, radio buttons, and dropdown menus are among the common form controls used to gather user input. Text fields allow users to enter text or numerical data, while checkboxes and radio buttons provide options for selecting single or multiple choices. Dropdown menus offer a list of selectable options in a scrollable format, enhancing the user experience when choosing from a set of predefined values.

Styling Forms with CSS

CSS (Cascading Style Sheets) plays a vital role in enhancing the visual presentation of HTML forms. By applying CSS styles to form elements, developers can customize the appearance, layout, and responsiveness of forms to align with the overall design of the webpage. CSS properties like background-color, border, padding, and margin can be used to modify the appearance of form fields, buttons, and the form container itself.

Moreover, CSS can be leveraged to create responsive forms that adapt to different screen sizes and devices, ensuring a consistent user experience across desktops, tablets, and smartphones. Techniques like flexbox and media queries enable developers to design forms that are visually appealing and user-friendly on various platforms.

By combining HTML forms with CSS styling, developers can create interactive and visually engaging forms that streamline user input and data submission processes. Understanding the principles of form design and styling empowers developers to build web pages that prioritize usability, accessibility, and aesthetic appeal, enhancing the overall user experience.

Organizing Content with Lists and Tables

In the realm of web development, organizing content efficiently is paramount for creating structured and user-friendly web pages. Two essential tools for structuring content in HTML are lists and tables, each serving distinct purposes in presenting information effectively to website visitors.

Creating Lists with <ol> and <ul> Tags

Lists in HTML are invaluable for categorizing and displaying content in an organized manner. There are two primary types of lists: ordered lists and unordered lists.

- **Ordered Lists (<ol>):** Ordered lists are used to present items in a sequential order, typically indicated by numbers or letters. The <ol> tag is employed to create an ordered list, with each list item defined by the <li> tag. Developers can customize the numbering style using CSS for enhanced visual appeal.

- **Unordered Lists (<ul>):** Unordered lists are ideal for showcasing items in a bulleted format without a specific sequence. The <ul> tag is utilized to generate an unordered list, with each item represented by the <li> tag. Bullets, squares, or custom symbols can be styled using CSS to differentiate list items.

By leveraging ordered and unordered lists, web developers can categorize and structure content logically, aiding in readability and user comprehension.

Constructing Tables with <table>, <tr>, <td>, and <th> Tags

Tables are instrumental in displaying data in a tabular format, making comparisons and relationships between different datasets more accessible. To build tables in HTML, several key tags are utilized:

- **<table>:** The <table> tag serves as the container for the entire table structure, defining the table boundaries and layout.

- **<tr>:** Within the <table> tag, rows are created using the <tr> tag to delineate horizontal groupings of table cells.

- **<td>:** Table data cells are declared with the <td> tag, representing individual data points within each row.

- **<th>:** Table header cells are designated by the <th> tag, typically used to label columns or rows in a table. Header cells are often styled differently from regular data cells for visual distinction.

By utilizing these table-related tags effectively, developers can present data in a tabular format that is visually structured and easily digestible for website visitors. Tables play a crucial role in organizing complex datasets, comparisons, and tabular information, enhancing the overall presentation of content on web pages.

Using Semantic HTML Elements

Semantic HTML elements play a crucial role in enhancing the structure and meaning of web content. Elements like <header>, <footer>, <article>, <section>, and <nav> provide valuable context to both browsers and developers, improving accessibility, SEO, and overall user experience.

Importance of Semantic HTML Elements

Semantic elements offer a clear and meaningful way to define the different parts of a webpage. For instance, the <header> element signifies the introductory content at the top of a page, while the <footer> element encapsulates the concluding details. By using semantic elements, developers can create well-organized and easily navigable websites that convey information effectively to users and search engines.

Usage of Key Semantic Elements

1. **<header>:** The <header> element typically contains introductory content, such as logos, navigation menus, and headings. It helps users identify the website and navigate its sections efficiently.

2. **<footer>:** Contrasting the header, the <footer> element denotes the end of a webpage and often includes copyright information, contact details, and additional links.

3. **<article>:** The <article> element defines a self-contained piece of content, such as a blog post, news article, or forum post. It allows search engines to recognize and index the main content accurately.

4. **<section>:** Sections are used to group related content within a webpage. They assist in structuring content hierarchically and improving the site's overall organization.

5. **<nav>:** The <nav> element is utilized for navigation links, menus, or any element directing users to other parts of the website. It aids in enhancing user experience and accessibility by providing clear navigation pathways.

Impact on SEO and Accessibility

Semantic HTML elements have a significant impact on SEO practices and accessibility standards. Search engines rely on structured content to understand the context and relevance of web pages. By using semantic elements correctly, developers can improve search engine rankings by providing clear indicators of content hierarchy and meaning.

In terms of accessibility, semantic elements assist screen readers and other assistive technologies in interpreting web content accurately. Users with disabilities rely on proper HTML semantics to navigate websites effectively. Semantic elements ensure that content is presented in a logical and understandable manner, enhancing accessibility for all users.

In conclusion, leveraging semantic HTML elements like <header>, <footer>, <article>, <section>, and <nav> is essential for creating well-structured, accessible, and SEO-friendly websites. By incorporating semantic elements thoughtfully, developers can enhance the user experience, improve search engine visibility, and promote inclusivity in web design practices.

HTML APIs and Document Object Model (DOM)

Introduce HTML APIs such as Canvas and Drag-and-Drop. Explain DOM, its tree-like structure, and how JavaScript can be used to manipulate HTML and CSS dynamically.

HTML APIs, such as Canvas and Drag-and-Drop, provide developers with powerful tools to enhance user interactions and create dynamic web experiences. The Canvas API allows for programmatically drawing graphics, animations, and other visual elements directly on a webpage, offering a versatile platform for creative expression and interactive content. On the other hand, the Drag-and-Drop API simplifies the implementation of drag-and-drop functionality, enabling users to intuitively move elements within a webpage.

One of the fundamental concepts in web development is the Document Object Model (DOM), which represents the structure of an HTML document as a hierarchical tree of objects. Each element in the DOM tree corresponds to a specific part of the HTML document, such as tags, attributes, and content. JavaScript, as a client-side scripting language, can interact with the DOM dynamically, allowing developers to manipulate HTML elements, update styles, and respond to user actions in real-time.

By leveraging JavaScript to access and modify the DOM, developers can create interactive web applications that respond to user input and update content dynamically. Through DOM manipulation, elements can be added, removed, or modified on the fly, enabling seamless updates to the webpage without requiring a full page refresh. This dynamic behavior enhances user engagement and interactivity, making web applications more responsive and engaging.

Understanding the DOM's tree-like structure is essential for efficiently traversing and manipulating elements within a webpage. Developers can access specific elements, modify their attributes, change styling properties, and respond to events using JavaScript. By combining HTML, CSS, and JavaScript, developers can create rich, interactive web experiences that adapt to user interactions and provide a fluid browsing experience across different devices and screen sizes.

In summary, HTML APIs like Canvas and Drag-and-Drop offer enhanced functionality for creating engaging web content, while the DOM provides a structured approach to dynamically interacting with HTML and CSS elements using JavaScript. Mastering these concepts empowers developers to build responsive and interactive web applications that captivate users and deliver immersive digital experiences.

HTML5 Innovations

HTML5 brought a wave of enhancements and new features that revolutionized web development. Among the standout additions were new elements like <canvas>, <figure>, and <figcaption>, which expanded the possibilities for creating interactive and visually engaging web content. The <canvas> element provided a powerful platform for dynamic graphics and animations, allowing developers to draw shapes, render images, and create intricate visual effects directly within the browser.

Furthermore, the <figure> and <figcaption> elements introduced semantic markup for images and multimedia content, enhancing accessibility and improving the structure of web documents. By encapsulating media elements within <figure> tags and providing descriptive captions with <figcaption>, developers could create more informative and well-organized web pages that catered to diverse user needs.

In addition to new elements, HTML5 introduced a range of innovative form control types that enhanced user input experiences. Features like date pickers, email validation, and input placeholders streamlined data entry and validation processes, improving usability and reducing errors in form submissions. These form control enhancements not only made web forms more user-friendly but also facilitated the collection of accurate and standardized data from visitors.

Another significant advancement in HTML5 was the introduction of HTML5 Web Storage, which provided developers with client-side storage options for storing data locally on users' devices. This feature enabled web applications to cache data, session information, and user preferences, reducing server load and enhancing offline functionality. By leveraging HTML5 Web Storage mechanisms like localStorage and sessionStorage, developers could create responsive and efficient web experiences that retained user data across browsing sessions.

Overall, HTML5 innovations, including new elements like <canvas>, <figure>, and `<figcaption>, advanced form control types, and HTML5 Web Storage, transformed the landscape of web development by offering enhanced capabilities for creating dynamic, interactive, and user-centric web applications. As developers continue to harness the power of HTML5 features, the potential for crafting immersive digital experiences and responsive web solutions grows, shaping the future of online content creation and user engagement.

Responsive Web Design with HTML and CSS

Responsive web design is a crucial aspect of modern web development, ensuring that websites adapt seamlessly to various devices and screen sizes. HTML and CSS work together harmoniously to create responsive designs that provide optimal user experiences across desktops, tablets, and smartphones. Let's delve into how HTML and CSS collaborate to achieve responsiveness through concepts like media queries, flexible grids, and viewports.

Media Queries for Adaptive Styling

Media queries in CSS enable developers to apply different styles based on the device's characteristics, such as screen width, height, and orientation. By using media queries within CSS, developers can target specific devices or screen sizes and adjust the layout, font sizes, and other design elements accordingly. Media queries allow for the creation of responsive designs that dynamically respond to the user's device, ensuring readability and usability across different platforms.

Flexible Grid Systems for Layout Flexibility

Flexible grid systems, often implemented using CSS frameworks like Bootstrap or Flexbox, provide a responsive layout structure that adapts to various screen sizes. Grid systems allow developers to define columns, rows, and breakpoints that reorganize content based on the available screen space. By utilizing flexible grids, developers can create fluid layouts that seamlessly adjust to different devices, maintaining visual consistency and readability across resolutions.

Viewport Meta Tag for Mobile Optimization

The viewport meta tag in HTML plays a vital role in optimizing websites for mobile devices. By setting the viewport meta tag with attributes like width=device-width and initial-scale=1, developers ensure that websites scale appropriately on mobile screens, preventing issues like zooming or horizontal scrolling. The viewport meta tag allows web pages to render correctly on smartphones and tablets, enhancing the mobile user experience and usability.

Incorporating media queries, flexible grids, and viewport meta tags into the HTML structure and CSS styling of a website lays the foundation for responsive web design. By leveraging these concepts effectively, developers can create websites that adapt fluidly to diverse devices, providing users with a seamless and engaging browsing experience. Responsive design not only improves accessibility and user satisfaction but also aligns with modern web standards, reflecting the ever-evolving landscape of digital technologies.

Optimizing HTML Pages for Search Engines

When it comes to maximizing the visibility and ranking of web pages on search engine results pages (SERPs), optimizing HTML content is paramount. Search Engine Optimization (SEO) involves various strategies and techniques to enhance a website's organic search performance, and optimizing HTML elements plays a crucial role in this process. By focusing on meta tags, consistent tag usage, and attributes like 'alt' for images, web developers can improve the SEO effectiveness of their HTML pages.

Meta Tags for Descriptive Metadata

Meta tags provide essential metadata about a webpage to search engines and website visitors. The meta elements, such as meta descriptions, meta keywords, and meta titles, offer concise summaries of the page's content, influencing search engine rankings and click-through rates. Including relevant keywords and descriptive text in meta tags helps search engines understand the page's context and relevance, improving its visibility in search results.

Consistent Use of Tags for Structure and Hierarchy

Consistency in using HTML tags for structuring content is vital for SEO. Search engines rely on well-defined structures within HTML documents to interpret and rank web pages accurately. By following best practices in tag usage, such as using heading tags (<h1> to <h6>) for titles and subheadings, developers can signal the hierarchy and importance of content to search engine crawlers. Maintaining a consistent tag hierarchy throughout the page ensures clarity and coherence, benefiting both SEO and user experience.

Utilizing 'Alt' Attributes for Image Optimization

Images are valuable assets for engaging users and enhancing visual appeal, but they also present SEO opportunities through proper optimization. The 'alt' attribute within the <img> tag provides alternative text for images, serving as a textual description for visually impaired users and search engine crawlers. Including relevant keywords in 'alt' text improves image search rankings and accessibility, making images more discoverable and contributing to overall SEO efforts.

By optimizing HTML pages with strategic meta tags, consistent tag usage, and descriptive 'alt' attributes for images, developers can enhance the visibility and searchability of their web content. Implementing these SEO best practices not only improves website rankings on search engines but also enhances user experience by providing clear, structured, and accessible content. Effective HTML optimization aligns with SEO guidelines and standards, empowering websites to attract more organic traffic and reach a wider online audience.

Debugging HTML Code Effectively

Debugging HTML code is an essential skill for web developers to ensure that websites function correctly and display content as intended. When encountering issues in HTML, understanding common problems and having effective debugging strategies can streamline the troubleshooting process. Here are some strategies and tools for debugging HTML code effectively:

Common HTML Issues and Resolutions

1. **Syntax Errors:** Syntax errors in HTML, such as missing closing tags or incorrect attribute values, can lead to rendering issues on web pages. To resolve syntax errors, developers should carefully review the code for typos, missing characters, or misplaced tags, ensuring that the HTML structure is well-formed and valid.

2. **CSS Styling Problems:** Incorrect CSS styling can impact the layout and appearance of HTML elements. Developers can use browser developer tools to inspect CSS properties applied to elements and identify styling conflicts or errors. Adjusting CSS rules and selectors can help resolve styling issues and improve the visual presentation of web pages.

3. **Broken Links:** Broken links, whether internal or external, can disrupt user navigation and hinder website functionality. Developers should regularly check links within HTML content to ensure they are valid and lead to the intended destinations. Using tools like link checkers can help identify broken links and address them promptly.

Tools for Debugging HTML Code

1. **Browser Developer Tools:** Most modern web browsers come equipped with developer tools that allow developers to inspect HTML elements, modify CSS styles, debug JavaScript code, and analyze network activity. By using browser developer tools, developers can troubleshoot HTML-related issues, test changes in real-time, and optimize website performance.

2. **HTML Validators:** Online HTML validators can help identify syntax errors, missing tags, and other HTML issues that may affect the rendering of web pages. Validating HTML code against standards like W3C (World Wide Web Consortium) specifications ensures compliance with best practices and enhances website accessibility and compatibility.

3. **Code Editors with Linting:** Code editors with built-in linting tools can automatically detect and highlight errors in HTML code, such as unclosed tags, redundant attributes, or deprecated elements. Linting features provide real-time feedback on coding practices, helping developers catch mistakes early and maintain clean, error-free HTML documents.

By employing these debugging strategies and utilizing tools like browser developer tools, HTML validators, and code editors with linting capabilities, developers can efficiently troubleshoot HTML code, address common issues, and optimize the performance and functionality of web pages. Debugging HTML effectively is crucial for delivering seamless user experiences and ensuring the quality and reliability of websites.

Future Trends in HTML

As web development continues to evolve, the landscape of HTML is poised for significant advancements and innovations. Professionals in the field should anticipate several key trends and developments that are likely to shape the future of HTML and web development.

1. Web Components and Custom Elements

Web components, a set of web platform APIs that allow for the creation of reusable custom elements, are expected to gain prominence in HTML development. With the use of custom elements, developers can encapsulate specific functionalities and design patterns into modular components, promoting code reusability and enhancing the maintainability of web projects.

2. Enhanced Accessibility Features

Accessibility is a critical aspect of modern web development, and HTML is likely to see improvements in native accessibility features. Future HTML standards may introduce enhanced support for accessibility attributes, ensuring that web content is more inclusive and usable for individuals with disabilities.

3. Integration of Machine Learning

The integration of machine learning capabilities directly into HTML could revolutionize how web applications operate. By leveraging machine learning models within HTML elements, developers may enable intelligent functionalities such as personalized content recommendations, predictive text input, and real-time data analysis.

4. Progressive Web Applications (PWAs)

The concept of Progressive Web Applications (PWAs) is expected to influence HTML development significantly. PWAs combine the best features of web and mobile applications, offering enhanced offline capabilities, push notifications, and app-like user experiences. HTML advancements may cater to the specific requirements of PWAs, enabling developers to create more robust and engaging web applications.

5. Embracing WebAssembly

WebAssembly, a binary instruction format for the web, opens up possibilities for high-performance web applications that rival native desktop software. HTML may integrate more seamlessly with WebAssembly, allowing developers to build complex applications like games, multimedia editors, and simulations directly within the browser environment.

6. Focus on Web Security

With the increasing focus on cybersecurity, HTML standards may introduce new security features to mitigate common web vulnerabilities. Enhanced security mechanisms within HTML elements could provide developers with tools to safeguard web applications against threats like cross-site scripting (XSS) and data breaches.

7. Augmented Reality (AR) and Virtual Reality (VR) Support

As AR and VR technologies gain traction, HTML is likely to incorporate native support for immersive experiences. Future HTML standards may include elements and APIs tailored for AR and VR content, enabling developers to create interactive and engaging virtual environments directly on the web.

In conclusion, the future of HTML holds exciting prospects for web developers, with advancements in web components, accessibility features, machine learning integration, PWAs, WebAssembly, web security, and AR/VR support reshaping the way web applications are built and experienced. Staying abreast of these emerging trends in HTML is essential for professionals looking to excel in the dynamic and ever-evolving realm of web development.

About HTML -----

Hyper Text Markup Language (HTML) is the standard markup language for documents designed to be displayed in a web browser. It defines the content and structure of web content. It is often assisted by technologies such as Cascading Style Sheets (CSS) and scripting languages such as JavaScript.

Web browsers receive HTML documents from a web server or from local storage and render the documents into multimedia web pages. HTML describes the structure of a web page semantically and originally included cues for its appearance.

HTML elements are the building blocks of HTML pages. With HTML constructs, images and other objects such as interactive forms may be embedded into the rendered page.

HTML provides a means to create structured documents by denoting structural semantics for text such as headings, paragraphs, lists, links, quotes, and other items.

HTML elements are delineated by *tags*, written using angle brackets. Tags such as **<img>** and **<input>** directly introduce content into the page.

Other tags such as **<p>** and **</p>** surround and provide information about document text and may include sub-element tags.

Browsers do not display the HTML tags but use them to interpret the content of the page.

HTML can embed programs written in a scripting language such as JavaScript, which affects the behavior and content of web pages.

The inclusion of CSS defines the look and layout of content.

The World Wide Web Consortium (W3C), former maintainer of the HTML and current maintainer of the CSS standards, has encouraged the use of CSS over explicit presentational HTML since 1997.

A form of HTML, known as HTML5, is used to display video and audio, primarily using the <canvas> element, together with JavaScript.

History Of HTML-----

Development

Tim Berners-Lee in April 2009

In 1980, physicist Tim Berners-Lee, a contractor at CERN, proposed and prototyped ENQUIRE, a system for CERN researchers to use and share documents.

In 1989, Berners-Lee wrote a memo proposing an Internet-based hypertext system. Berners-Lee specified HTML and wrote the browser and server software in late 1990.

That year, Berners-Lee and CERN data systems engineer Robert Cailliau collaborated on a joint request for funding, but the project was not formally adopted by CERN.

In his personal notes of 1990, Berners-Lee listed "some of the many areas in which hypertext is used"; an encyclopedia is the first entry.

The first publicly available description of HTML was a document called "HTML Tags", first mentioned on the Internet by Tim Berners-Lee in late 1991.

It describes 18 elements comprising the initial, relatively simple design of HTML. Except for the hyperlink tag, these were strongly influenced by SGMLguid, an in-house Standard Generalized Markup Language (SGML)-based documentation format at CERN. Eleven of these elements still exist in HTML 4.

HTML is a markup language that web browsers use to interpret and compose text, images, and other material into visible or audible web pages. Default characteristics for every item of HTML markup are defined in the browser, and these characteristics can be altered or enhanced by the web page designer's additional use of CSS.

Many of the text elements are mentioned in the 1988 ISO technical report TR 9537 *Techniques for using SGML*, which describes the features of early text formatting languages such as that used by the RUNOFF command developed in the early 1960s for the CTSS (Compatible Time-Sharing System) operating system. These formatting commands were derived from the commands used by typesetters to manually format documents. However, the SGML concept of generalized markup is based on elements (nested annotated ranges with attributes) rather than merely print effects, with separate structure and markup.

HTML has been progressively moved in this direction with CSS. Berners-Lee considered HTML to be an application of SGML.

It was formally defined as such by the Internet Engineering Task Force (IETF) with the mid-1993 publication of the first proposal for an HTML specification, the "Hypertext Markup Language (HTML)" Internet Draft by Berners-Lee and Dan Connolly, which included an SGML Document type definition to define the syntax.

The draft expired after six months, but was notable for its acknowledgment of the NCSA Mosaic browser's custom tag for embedding in-line images, reflecting the IETF's philosophy of basing standards on successful prototypes. Similarly, Dave Raggett's competing Internet Draft, "HTML+ (Hypertext Markup Format)", from late 1993, suggested standardizing already-implemented features like tables and fill-out forms.

After the HTML and HTML+ drafts expired in early 1994, the IETF created an HTML Working Group. In 1995, this working group completed "HTML 2.0", the first HTML specification intended to be treated as a standard against which future implementations should be based.

Further development under the auspices of the IETF was stalled by competing interests. Since 1996, the HTML specifications have been maintained, with input from commercial software vendors, by the World Wide Web Consortium (W3C).

In 2000, HTML became an international standard (ISO/IEC 15445:2000). HTML 4.01 was published in late 1999, with further errata published through 2001. In 2004, development began on HTML5 in the Web Hypertext Application

Technology Working Group (WHATWG), which became a joint deliverable with the W3C in 2008, and was completed and standardized on 28 October 2014.

HTML Versions Timeline -----

- **1991-** Tim Berners-Lee invents HTML 1.0

- **1993-** HTML 1.0 is released. Not many developers are creating websites at this time.

- **1995-** HTML 2.0 is published. This contains the features of HTML 1.0 plus new features. This remained the standard markup language for designing and creating websites until 1997.

- **1997-** HTML 3.0 was invented. Here, Dave Raggett introduced a fresh draft on HTML, which improved new features of HTML and gave more powerful characteristics for webmasters in designing websites. Unfortunately, the powerful features slowed down the browser in applying further improvements.

- **1999-** The widely-used HTML 4.0 comes out. It is very successful.

- **2014-** HTML 5.0 is released and used worldwide. It is said to be the extended version of HTML 4.01 which was published in 2012.

LOGO OF HTML5....

HTML5: The Modern Standard -----

HTML5 is the fifth major version of HTML. It emerged as the modern standard for web development. It aimed to address the limitations of previous versions, introduce new features, and provide a more powerful and flexible platform for creating web content.

Features of HTML5

- Enhanced Interactivity: HTML5 introduced new APIs and scripting capabilities that enabled developers to create interactive web applications. These APIs included features for drag and drop, geolocation, canvas for drawing graphics, and WebSockets for real-time communication.

- Mobile Compatibility: HTML5 was designed with mobile devices in mind, aiming to provide better support and responsiveness across different screen sizes and touch interactions. It facilitated the development of mobile-friendly websites and web applications.

- Semantic Elements: HTML5 introduced semantic elements such as

  ,,,,,, and. These elements provided clearer structural meaning to web content, aiding accessibility and search engine optimization.

- Audio and Video Elements: HTML5 introduced the

  - Canvas Element: HTML5 introduced the

  - Form Enhancements: HTML5 introduced new input types and attributes for form fields, such as email, URL, date, time, and range. It also introduced the

  - Scalable Vector Graphics (SVG): HTML5 included native support for SVG, a powerful graphics format that allowed for the creation of scalable vector-based images and animations. SVG graphics could be integrated directly into HTML5 documents.

- Media Streaming: HTML5 introduced support for streaming audio and video content, enabling real-time playback of media without the need for external applications or plugins.

- Mobile-Friendly Markup: HTML5 introduced elements and attributes that facilitated the development of mobile-friendly web pages. These included the

  element for navigation menus, the ☐ type for mobile-specific input controls, and the viewport tag for controlling how web content is displayed on mobile devices.

- Responsive Web Design: HTML5 embraced responsive design principles by providing flexible layout options. CSS media queries allowed developers to adapt the layout and styling of web content based on the device's screen size and resolution.

- Touch Events: HTML5 introduced touch event APIs, enabling developers to create interactive touch-based interactions in web applications, such as swipe gestures, pinch-to-zoom, and multi-touch gestures.

- Geolocation: HTML5 provided native support for obtaining the user's geographical location through the Geolocation API. This allowed developers to create location-aware web applications and provide location-based services.

HTML5 revolutionized web development by introducing new elements, enhanced multimedia capabilities, support for mobile devices, and the foundation for responsive design. Its features and flexibility have made it the standard for modern web development, enabling richer and more interactive web experiences.

- Canvas Element: HTML5 introduced the

- Form Enhancements: HTML5 introduced new input types and attributes for form fields, such as email, URL, date, time, and range. It also introduced the

- Scalable Vector Graphics (SVG): HTML5 included native support for SVG, a powerful graphics format that allowed for the creation of scalable vector-based images and animations. SVG graphics could be integrated directly into HTML5 documents.

- Media Streaming: HTML5 introduced support for streaming audio and video content, enabling real-time playback of media without the need for external applications or plugins.

- Mobile-Friendly Markup: HTML5 introduced elements and attributes that facilitated the development of mobile-friendly web pages. These included the

  element for navigation menus, the ⌐ type for mobile-specific input controls, and theviewport tag for controlling how web content is displayed on mobile devices.

- Responsive Web Design: HTML5 embraced responsive design principles by providing flexible layout options. CSS media queries allowed developers to adapt the layout and styling of web content based on the device's screen size and resolution.

- Touch Events: HTML5 introduced touch event APIs, enabling developers to create interactive touch-based interactions in web applications, such as swipe gestures, pinch-to-zoom, and multi-touch gestures.

- Geolocation: HTML5 provided native support for obtaining the user's geographical location through the Geolocation API. This allowed developers to create location-aware web applications and provide location-based services.

HTML5 revolutionized web development by introducing new elements, enhanced multimedia capabilities, support for mobile devices, and the foundation for responsive design. Its features and flexibility have made it the standard for modern web development, enabling richer and more interactive web experiences.

HTML6 and Potential Advancements -----

While there is currently no official HTML6 specification, discussions and proposals for potential advancements in the future of HTML are ongoing.

The potential areas of advancement include:

- **Enhanced Layout and Styling:** Efforts are being made to improve HTML's layout capabilities, allowing for more sophisticated and flexible page layouts without relying heavily on CSS frameworks or external libraries. This may include features like grid-based layout systems and improved handling of responsive design.

- **Improved Performance and Efficiency:** HTML may see advancements focused on optimizing performance and reducing page load times. This could involve introducing features that enhance caching, minimize code redundancy, and improve resource management.

- **Expanded Web Application Capabilities:** HTML may continue to evolve as a platform for building web applications. This may involve introducing new APIs, enhanced support for client-side storage, offline capabilities, and native integration with emerging technologies like WebRTC (Real-Time Communication) and WebAssembly.

- **Enhanced Security and Privacy:** The future of HTML may include additional features and APIs aimed at strengthening security and privacy on the web. This could involve improvements in cross-origin security, better protection against common web vulnerabilities, and enhanced mechanisms for user privacy and data protection.

As HTML continues to evolve, it will strive to address the changing needs of web development, improve performance and efficiency, and embrace emerging technologies. The future of HTML is focused on providing developers with a powerful and versatile platform for creating engaging, accessible, and secure web experiences.

A Change -----

Included in this chapter is information on:

- How the World Wide Web began
- The events and circumstances that led to the World Wide Web's current popularity
- How HTML has grown from its conception in the early 1990s

Summary

HTML has had a life-span of roughly seven years. During that time, it has evolved from a simple language with a small number of tags to a complex system of mark-up, enabling authors to create all-singing-and-dancing Web pages complete with animated images, sound and all manner of gimmicks. This chapter tells you something about the Web's early days, HTML, and about the people, companies and organizations who contributed to HTML+, HTML 2, HTML 3.2 and finally, HTML 4.

This chapter is a short history of HTML. Its aim is to give readers some idea of how the HTML we use today was developed from the prototype written by Tim Berners-Lee in 1992. The story is interesting - not least because HTML has been through an extremely bumpy ride on the road to standardization, with software engineers, academics and browser companies haggling about the language like so many Ministers of Parliament debating in the House of Commons.

1989: Tim Berners-Lee invents the Web with HTML as its publishing language

The World Wide Web began life in the place where you would least expect it: at CERN, the European Laboratory for Particle Physics in Geneva, Switzerland. CERN is a meeting place for physicists from all over the world, where highly abstract and conceptual thinkers engage in the contemplation of complex atomic phenomena that occur on a minuscule scale in time and space. This is a surprising place indeed for the beginnings of a technology which would, eventually, deliver everything from tourist information, online shopping and advertisements, financial data, weather forecasts and much more to your personal computer.

Tim Berners-Lee is the inventor of the Web. In 1989, Tim was working in a computing services section of CERN when he came up with the concept; at the time he had no idea that it would be implemented on such an enormous scale. Particle physics research often involves collaboration among institutes from all over the world. Tim had the idea of enabling researchers from remote sites in the world to organize and pool together information. But far from simply making available a large number of research documents as files that could be downloaded to individual computers, he suggested that you could actually link the text in the files themselves.

In other words, there could be cross-references from one research paper to another. This would mean that while reading one research paper, you could quickly display part of another paper that holds directly relevant text or diagrams. Documentation of a scientific and mathematical nature would thus be represented as a `web' of information held in electronic form on computers across the world. This, Tim thought, could be done by using some form of hypertext, some way of linking documents together by using buttons on the screen, which you simply clicked on to jump from one paper to another. Before coming to CERN, Tim had already worked on document production and text processing, and had developed his first hypertext system, `Enquire', in 1980 for his own personal use.

Tim's prototype Web browser on the NeXT computer came out in 1990.

Through 1990: The time was ripe for Tim's invention

The fact that the Web was invented in the early 1990s was no coincidence. Developments in communications technology during that time meant that, sooner or later, something like the Web was bound to happen. For a start, *hypertext* was coming into vogue and being used on computers. Also, Internet users were gaining in the number of users on the system: there was an increasing audience for distributed information. Last, but not least, the new domain name system had made it much easier to address a machine on the Internet.

Hypertext

lthough already established as a concept by academics as early as the 1940s, it was with the advent of the personal computer that hypertext came out of the cupboard. In the late 1980s, Bill Atkinson, an exceptionally gifted programmer working for Apple Computer Inc., came up with an application called *Hypercard* for the Macintosh. Hypercard enabled you to construct a series of on-screen 'filing cards' that contained textual and graphical information. Users could navigate these by pressing on-screen buttons, taking themselves on a tour of the information in the process.

Hypercard set the scene for more applications based on the filing card idea. Toolbook for the PC was used in the early 1990s for constructing hypertext training courses that had 'pages' with buttons which could go forward or backward or jump to a new topic. Behind the scenes, buttons would initiate little programs called scripts. These scripts would control which page would be presented next; they could even run a small piece of animation on the screen. The application entitled Guide was a similar application for UNIX and the PC.

Hypercard and its imitators caught the popular imagination. However, these packages still had one major limitation: hypertext jumps could only be made to files on the same computer. Jumps made to computers on the other side of the world were still out of the question. Nobody yet had implemented a system involving hypertext links on a global scale.

The domain name system

By the middle 1980s, the Internet had a new, easy-to-use system for naming computers. This involved using the idea of the domain name. A domain name comprises a series of letters separated by dots, for example: 'www.bo.com' or 'www.erb.org.uk'. These names are the easy-to-use alternative to the much less manageable and cumbersome IP address numbers.

A program called Distributed Name Service (DNS) maps domain names onto IP addresses, keeping the IP addresses 'hidden'. DNS was an absolute breakthrough in making the Internet accessible to those who were not computer nerds. As a result of its introduction, email addresses became simpler. Previous to DNS, email addresses had all sorts of hideous codes such as exclamation marks, percent signs and other extraneous information to specify the route to the other machine.

Choosing the right approach to create a global hypertext system

To Tim Berners-Lee, global hypertext links seemed feasible, but it was a matter of finding the correct approach to implementing them. Using an existing hypertext package might seem an attractive proposition, but this was impractical for a number of reasons. To start with, any hypertext tool to be used worldwide would have to take into account that many types of computers existed that were linked to the Internet: Personal Computers, Macintoshes, UNIX machines and simple terminals. Also, many desktop publishing methods were in vogue: SGML, Interleaf, LaTex, Microsoft Word, and Troff among many others. Commercial hypertext packages were computer-specific and could not easily take text from other sources; besides, they were far too complicated and involved tedious compiling of text into internal formats to create the final hypertext system.

What was needed was something very simple, at least in the beginning. Tim demonstrated a basic, but attractive way of publishing text by developing some software himself, and also his own simple protocol - HTTP - for retrieving other documents' text via hypertext links. Tim's own protocol, HTTP, stands for HyperText Transfer Protocol. The text format for HTTP was named HTML, for HyperText Mark-up Language; Tim's hypertext implementation was demonstrated on a NeXT workstation, which provided many of the tools he needed to develop his first prototype. By keeping things very simple, Tim encouraged others to build upon his ideas and to design further software for displaying HTML, and for setting up their own HTML documents ready for access.

Tim bases his HTML on an existing internationally agreed upon method of text mark-up

The HTML that Tim invented was strongly based on SGML (Standard Generalized Mark-up Language), an internationally agreed upon method for marking up text into structural units such as paragraphs, headings, list items and so on. SGML could be implemented on any machine. The idea was that the language was independent of the formatter (the browser or other viewing software) which actually displayed the text on the screen. The use of pairs of tags such as <TITLE> and </TITLE> is taken directly from SGML, which does exactly the same. The SGML elements used in Tim's HTML included P (paragraph); H1 through H6 (heading level 1 through heading level 6); OL (ordered lists); UL (unordered lists); LI (list items) and various others. What

SGML does not include, of course, are hypertext links: the idea of using the anchor element with the HREF attribute was purely Tim's invention, as was the now-famous `www.name.name' format for addressing machines on the Web.

Basing HTML on SGML was a brilliant idea: other people would have invented their own language from scratch but this might have been much less reliable, as well as less acceptable to the rest of the Internet community. Certainly the simplicity of HTML, and the use of the anchor element A for creating hypertext links, was what made Tim's invention so useful.

September 1991: Open discussion about HTML across the Internet begins

Far from keeping his ideas private, Tim made every attempt to discuss them openly online across the Internet. Coming from a research background, this was quite a natural thing to do. In September 1991, the WWW-talk mailing list was started, a kind of electronic discussion group in which enthusiasts could exchange ideas and gossip. By 1992, a handful of other academics and computer researchers were showing interest. Dave Raggett from Hewlett-Packard's Labs in Bristol, England, was one of these early enthusiasts, and, following electronic discussion, Dave visited Tim in 1992.

Here, in Tim's tiny room in the bowels of the sprawling buildings of CERN, the two engineers further considered how HTML might be taken from its current beginnings and shaped into something more appropriate for mass consumption. Trying to anticipate the kind of features that users really would like, Dave looked through magazines, newspapers and other printed media to get an idea of what sort of HTML features would be important when that same information was published online. Upon return to England, Dave sat down at his keyboard and resolutely composed HTML+, a richer version of the original HTML.

Late 1992: NCSA is intrigued by the idea of the Web

Meanwhile on the other side of the world, Tim's ideas had caught the eye of Joseph Hardin and Dave Thompson, both of the National Center for Supercomputer Applications, a research institute at the University of Illinois at Champaign-Urbana. They managed to connect to the computer at CERN and download copies of two free Web browsers. Realizing the importance of what they saw, NCSA decided to develop a browser of their own to be called *Mosaic*. Among the programmers in the NCSA team were Marc Andreessen - who later made his millions by selling Web products - and the brilliant programmer Eric Bina - who also became rich, courtesy of the Web. Eric Bina was a kind of software genius who reputedly could stay up three nights in succession, typing in a reverie of hacking at his computer.

December 1992: Marc Andreessen makes a brief appearance on WWW- talk

Early Web enthusiasts exchanged ideas and gossip over an electronic discussion group called WWW-talk. This was where Dave Raggett, Tim Berners-Lee, Dan Connolly and others debated how images (photographs, diagrams, illustrations and so on) should be inserted into HTML documents. Not everyone agreed upon the way that the relevant tag should be implemented, or even what that tag should be called. Suddenly, Marc Andreessen appeared on WWW-talk and, without further to-do, introduced an idea for the IMG tag by the Mosaic team.

It was quite plain that the others were not altogether keen on the design of IMG, but Andreessen was not easily redirected. The IMG tag was implemented in the form suggested by the Mosaic team on its browser and remains to this day firmly implanted in HTML. This was much to the chagrin of supporters back in academia who invented several alternatives to IMG in the years to come. Now, with the coming of HTML 4, the OBJECT tag potentially replaces IMG, but this is, of course, some years later.

March 1993: Lou Montulli releases the Lynx browser version 2.0a

Lou Montulli was one of the first people to write a text-based browser, Lynx. The Lynx browser was a text-based browser for terminals and for computers that used DOS without Windows. Lou Montulli was later recruited to work with Netscape Communications Corp., but nonetheless remained partially loyal to the idea of developing HTML as an open standard, proving a real asset to the HTML working group and the HTML Editorial Board in years to come. Lou's enthusiasm for good, expensive wine, and his knowledge of excellent restaurants in the Silicon Valley area were to make the standardization of HTML a much more pleasurable process.

Early 1993: Dave Raggett begins to write his own browser

While Eric Bina and the NCSA Mosaic gang were hard at it hacking through the night, Dave Raggett of Hewlett-Packard Labs in Bristol was working part-time on his Arena browser, on which he hoped to demonstrate all sorts of newly invented features for HTML.

April 1993: The Mosaic browser is released

In April 1993, version 1 of the Mosaic browser was released for Sun Microsystems Inc.'s workstation, a computer used in software development running the UNIX operating system. Mosaic extended the features specified by Tim Berners-Lee; for example, it added images, nested lists and fill-out forms. Academics and software engineers later would argue that many of these extensions were very much ad hoc and not properly designed.

Late 1993: Large companies underestimate the importance of the Web

Dave Raggett's work on the Arena browser was slow because he had to develop much of it single-handedly: no money was available to pay for a team of developers. This was because Hewlett-Packard, in common with many other large computer companies, was quite unconvinced that the Internet would be a success; indeed, the need for a global hypertext system simply passed them by. For many large corporations, the question of whether or not any money could be made from the Web was unclear from the outset.

There was also a misconception that the Internet was mostly for academics. In some companies, senior management was assured that the telephone companies would provide the technology for global communications of this sort, anyway. The result was that individuals working in research labs in the commercial sector were unable to devote much time to Web development. This was a bitter disappointment to some researchers, who gratefully would have committed nearly every waking moment toward shaping what they envisioned would be *the* communications system of the future.

Dave Raggett, realizing that there were not enough working hours left for him to succeed at what he felt was an immensely important task, continued writing his browser at home. There he would sit at a large computer that occupied a fair portion of the dining room table, sharing its slightly sticky surface with paper, crayons, Lego bricks and bits of half-eaten cookies left by the children. Dave also used the browser to show text flow around images, forms and other aspects of HTML at the First WWW Conference in Geneva in 1994. The Arena browser was later used for development work at CERN.

May 1994: NCSA assigns commercial rights for Mosaic browser to Spyglass, Inc.

In May 1994, Spyglass, Inc. signed a multi-million dollar licensing agreement with NCSA to distribute a commercially enhanced version of Mosaic. In August of that same year, the University of Illinois at Champaign-Urbana, the home of NCSA, assigned all future commercial rights for NCSA Mosaic to Spyglass.

May 1994: The first World Wide Web conference is held in Geneva, with HTML+ on show

Although Marc Andreessen and Jim Clark had commercial interests in mind, the rest of the World Wide Web community had quite a different attitude: they saw themselves as joint creators of a wonderful new technology, which certainly would benefit the world. They were jiggling with excitement. Even quiet and retiring academics became animated in discussion, and many seemed evangelical about their new-found god of the Web.

At the first World Wide Web conference organized by CERN in May 1994, all was merry with 380 attendees - who mostly were from Europe but also included many from the United States. You might have thought that Marc Andreessen, Jim Clark and Eric Bina surely would be there, but they were not. For the most part, participants were from the academic community, from institutions such as the World Meteorological Organization, the International Center for Theoretical Physics, the University of Iceland and so on. Later conferences had much more of a commercial feel, but this one was for technical enthusiasts who instinctively knew that this was the start of something big.

At the World Wide Web conference in Geneva. Left to right: Joseph Hardin from NCSA, Robert Cailliau from CERN, Tim Berners-Lee from CERN and Dan Connolly (of HTML 2 fame) then working for Hal software.

During the course of that week, awards were presented for notable achievements on the Web; these awards were given to Marc Andreessen, Lou Montulli, Eric Bina, Rob Hartill and Kevin Hughes. Dan Connolly, who proceeded to define HTML 2, gave a slide presentation entitled *Interoperability: Why Everyone Wins*, which explained why it was important that the Web operated with a proper HTML specification. Strange to think that at least three of the people who received awards at the conference were later to fly in the face of Dan's idea that adopting a cross-company uniform standard for HTML was essential.

Dave Raggett had been working on some new HTML ideas, which he called HTML+. At the conference it was agreed that the work on HTML+ should be carried forward to lead to the development of an HTML 3 standard. Dave Raggett, together with CERN, developed Arena further as a proof-of-concept browser for this work. Using Arena, Dave Raggett, Henrik Frystyk Nielsen, Håkon Lie and others demonstrated text flow around a figure with captions, resizable tables, image backgrounds, math and other features.

A panel discussion at the Geneva conference. Kevin Altis from Intel, Dave Raggett from HP Labs, Rick `Channing' Rodgers from the National Library of Medicine.

The conference ended with a glorious evening cruise on board a paddle steamer around Lake Geneva with *Wolfgang and the Werewolves* providing Jazz accompaniment.

September 1994: The Internet Engineering Task Force (IETF) sets up an HTML working group

In early 1994, an Internet Engineering Task Force working group was set up to deal with HTML.

His Internet Engineering Task Force is the international standards and development body of the Internet and is a large, open community of network designers, operators, vendors and researchers concerned with the evolution and smooth operation of the Internet architecture. The technical work of the IETF is done in working groups, which are organized by topic into several areas; for example, security, network routing, and applications. The IETF is, in general, part of a culture that sees the Internet as belonging to The People. This was even more so in the early days of the Web.

His feelings of the good `ole days of early Web development are captured in the song, *The Net Flag*, which can be found `somewhere on the Internet'. The first verse runs as follows:

The people's web is deepest red,
And oft it's killed our routers dead.
But ere the bugs grew ten days old,
The patches fixed the broken code.

Chorus:

So raise the open standard high
Within its codes we'll live or die
Though cowards flinch and Bill Gates sneers
We'll keep the net flag flying here.

In keeping with normal IETF practices, the HTML working group was open to anyone in the engineering community: any interested computer scientist could potentially become a member and, once on its mailing list, could take part in email debate. The HTML working group met approximately three times a year, during which time they would enjoy a good haggle about HTML features present and future, be pleasantly suffused with coffee and beer, striding about plush hotel lobbies sporting pony tails, T-shirts and jeans without the slightest care.

July 1994: HTML specification for HTML 2 is released

During 1993 and early 1994, lots of browsers had added their own bits to HTML; the language was becoming ill-defined. In an effort to make sense of the chaos, Dan Connolly and colleagues collected all the HTML tags that were widely used and collated them into a draft document that defined the breadth of what Tim Berners-Lee called HTML 2. The draft was then circulated through the Internet community for comment. With the patience of a saint, Dan took into account numerous suggestions from HTML enthusiasts far and wide, ensuring that all would be happy with the eventual HTML 2 definition. He also wrote a Document Type Definition for HTML 2, a kind of mathematically precise description of the language.

November 1994: Netscape is formed

During 1993, Marc Andreessen apparently felt increasingly irritated at simply being *on* the Mosaic project rather than in charge of it. Upon graduating, he decided to leave NCSA and head for California where he met Jim Clark, who was already well known in Silicon Valley and who had money to invest. Together they formed Mosaic Communications, which then became Netscape Communications Corp. in November, 1994. What they planned to do was create and market their very own browser.

The browser they designed was immensely successful - so much so in fact, that for some time to come, many users would mistakenly think that Netscape invented the Web. Netscape did its best to make sure that even those who were relying on a low-bandwidth connection - that is, even those who only had a modem-link from a home personal computer - were able to access the Web effectively. This was greatly to the company's credit.

Following a predictable path, Netscape began inventing its own HTML tags as it pleased without first openly discussing them with the Web community. Netscape rarely made an appearance at the big International WWW conferences, but it seemed to be driving the HTML standard. It was a curious situation, and one that the inner core of the HTML community felt they must redress.

Late 1994: The World Wide Web Consortium forms

The World Wide Web Consortium was formed in late 1994 to fulfill the potential of the Web through the development of open standards. They had a strong interest in HTML. Just as an orchestra insists on the best musicians, so the consortium recruited many of the best-known names in the Web community. Headed up by Tim Berners-Lee, here are just some of the players in the band today (1997):

Members of the World Wide Web Consortium at the MIT site. From left to right are Henrick Frystyk Neilsen, Anselm Baird-Smith, Jay Sekora, Rohit Khare, Dan Connolly, Jim Gettys, Tim Berners-Lee, Susan Hardy, Jim Miller, Dave Raggett, Tom Greene, Arthur Secret, Karen MacArthur.

- Dave Raggett on HTML; from the United Kingdom.
- Arnaud le Hors on HTML; from France.
- Dan Connolly on HTML; from the United States.
- Henrik Frystyk Nielsen on HTTP and on enabling the Web to go faster; from Denmark.
- Håkon Lie on style sheets; from Norway. He is located in France, working at INRIA.
- Bert Bos on style sheets and layout; from the Netherlands.
- Jim Miller on investigating technologies that could be used in rating the content of Web pages; from the United States.
- Chris Lilley on style sheets and font support; from the United Kingdom.

The W3 Consortium is based in part at the Laboratory of Computer Science at Massachusetts' Institute of Technology in Cambridge, Massachusetts, in the United States; and in part at INRIA, the *Institut National de Recherche en Informatique et en Automatique*, a French governmental research institute. The W3 Consortium is also located in part at Keio University in Japan. You can look at the Consortium's Web pages on `www.w3.org'.

The consortium is sponsored by a number of companies that directly benefit from its work on standards and other technology for the Web. The member companies include Digital Equipment Corp.; Hewlett-Packard Co.; IBM Corp.; Microsoft Corp.; Netscape Communications Corp.; and Sun Microsystems Inc., among many others.

Through 1995: HTML is extended with many new tags

During 1995, all kinds of new HTML tags emerged. Some, like the BGCOLOR attribute of the BODY element and FONT FACE, which control stylistic aspects of a document, found themselves in the black books of the academic engineering community. `You're not supposed to be able to do things like that in HTML,' they would protest. It was their belief that such things as text color, background texture, font size and font face were definitely outside the scope of a language when their only intent was to specify how a document would be organized.

March 1995: HTML 3 is published as an Internet Draft

Dave Raggett had been working for some time on his new ideas for HTML, and at last he formalized them in a document published as an Internet Draft in March, 1995. All manner of HTML features were covered. A new tag for inserting images called FIG was introduced, which Dave hoped would supersede IMG, as well as a whole gambit of features for marking up math and scientific documents. Dave dealt with HTML tables and tabs, footnotes and forms. He also added support for style sheets by including a STYLE tag and a CLASS attribute. The latter was to be available on every element to encourage authors to give HTML elements styles, much as you do in desktop publishing.

Although the HTML 3 draft was very well received, it was somewhat difficult to get it ratified by the IETF. The belief was that the draft was too large and too full of new proposals. To get consensus on a draft 150 pages long and about which everyone wanted to voice an opinion was optimistic - to say the least. In the end, Dave and the inner circle of the HTML community decided to call it a day.

Of course, browser writers were very keen on supporting HTML 3 - in theory. Inevitably, each browser writer chose to implement a different subset of HTML 3's features as they were so inclined, and then proudly proclaimed to support the standard. The confusion was mind-boggling, especially as browsers even came out with *extensions* to HTML 3, implying to the ordinary gent that *normal* HTML 3 was, of course, already supported. Was there an official HTML 3 standard or not? The truth was that there was not, but reading the computer press you might never have known the difference.

March 1995: A furor over the HTML Tables specification

Dave Raggett's HTML 3 draft had tackled the tabular organization of information in HTML. Arguments over this aspect of the language had continued for some time, but now it was time to really get going. At the 32nd meeting of the IETF in Danvers, Massachusetts, Dave found a group from the SGML brethren who were up in arms over part of the tables specification because it contradicted the CALS table model. Groups such as the US Navy use the CALS table model in complex documentation. After long negotiation, Dave managed to placate the CALS table delegates and altered the draft to suit their needs. HTML tables, which were not in HTML originally, finally surfaced from the HTML 3 draft to appear in HTML 3.2. They continue to be used extensively for the purpose of providing a layout grid for organizing pictures and text on the screen.

August 1995: Microsoft's Internet Explorer browser comes out

Version 1.0 of Microsoft Corp.'s Internet Explorer browser was announced. This browser was eventually to compete with Netscape's browser, and to evolve its own HTML features. To a certain extent, Microsoft built its business on the Web by extending HTML features. The ActiveX feature made Microsoft's browser unique, and Netscape developed a plug-in called Ncompass to handle ActiveX. This whole idea whereby one browser experiments with an extension to HTML only to find others adding support to keep even, continues to the present.

In November 1995, Microsoft's Internet Explorer version 2.0 arrived for its Windows NT and Windows 95 operating systems.

September 1995: Netscape submits a proposal for frames

By this time, Netscape submitted a proposal for frames, which involved the screen being divided into independent, scrollable areas. The proposal was implemented on Netscape's Navigator browser before anyone really had time to comment on it, but nobody was surprised.

November 1995: The HTML working group runs into problems

The HTML working group was an excellent idea in theory, but in practice things did not go quite as expected. With the immense popularity of the Web, the HTML working group grew larger and larger, and the volume of associated email soared exponentially. Imagine one hundred people trying to design a house. `I want the windows to be double-glazed,' says one. `Yes, but shouldn't we make them smaller, while we're at it,' questions another. Still others chime in: `What material do you propose for the frames - I'm not having them in plastic, that's for sure'; `I suggest that we don't have windows, as such, but include small, circular port-holes on the Southern elevation...' and so on.

You get the idea. The HTML working group emailed each other in a frenzy of electronic activity. In the end, its members became so snowed under with email that no time was left for programming. For software engineers, this was a sorry state of affairs, indeed: `I came back after just three days away to find over 2000 messages waiting,' was the unhappy lament of the HTML enthusiast.

Anyway, the HTML working group still was losing ground to the browser vendors. The group was notably slow in coming to a consensus on a given HTML feature, and commercial organizations were hardly going to sit around having tea, pleasantly conversing on the weather whilst waiting for the results of debates. And they did not.

November 1995: Vendors unite to form a new group dedicated to developing an HTML standard

In November, 1995 Dave Raggett called together representatives of the browser companies and suggested they meet as a small group dedicated to standardizing HTML. Imagine his surprise when it worked! Lou Montulli from Netscape, Charlie Kindel from Microsoft, Eric Sink from Spyglass, Wayne Gramlich from Sun Microsystems, Dave Raggett, Tim Berners-Lee and Dan Connolly from the W3 Consortium, and Jonathan Hirschman from Pathfinder convened near Chicago and made quick and effective decisions about HTML.

November 1995: Style sheets for HTML documents begin to take shape

Bert Bos, Håkon Lie, Dave Raggett, Chris Lilley and others from the World Wide Web Consortium and others met in Versailles near Paris to discuss the deployment of Cascading Style Sheets. The name Cascading Style Sheets implies that more than one style sheet can interact to produce the final look of the document. Using a special language, the CSS group advocated that everyone would soon be able to write simple styles for HTML, as one would do in Microsoft Word and other desktop publishing software packages. The SGML contingent, who preferred a LISP-like language called DSSSL - it rhymes with whistle - seemed out of the race when Microsoft promised to implement CSS on its Internet Explorer browser.

November 1995: Internationalization of HTML Internet Draft

Gavin Nicol, Gavin Adams and others presented a long paper on the internationalization of the Web. Their idea was to extend the capabilities of HTML 2, primarily by removing the restriction on the character set used. This would mean that HTML could be used to mark up languages other than those that use the Latin-1 character set to include a wider variety of alphabets and character sets, such as those that read from right to left.

December 1995: The HTML working group is dismantled

Since the IETF HTML working group was having difficulties coming to consensus swiftly enough to cope with such a fast-evolving standard, it was eventually dismantled.

February 1996: The HTML ERB is formed

Following the success of the November, 1995 meeting, the World Wide Web Consortium formed the HTML Editorial Review Board to help with the standardization process. This board consisted of representatives from IBM, Microsoft, Netscape, Novell, Softquad and the W3 Consortium, and did its business via telephone conference and email exchanges, meeting approximately once every three months. Its aim was to collaborate and agree upon a common standard for HTML, thus putting an end to the era when browsers each implemented a different subset of the language. The bad fairy of incompatibility was to be banished from the HTML kingdom forever, or one could hope so, perhaps.

Dan Connolly of the W3 Consortium, also author of HTML 2, deftly accomplished the feat of chairing what could be quite a raucous meeting of the clans. Dan managed to make sure that all representatives had their say and listened to each other's point of view in an orderly manner. A strong chair was absolutely essential in these meetings.

In preparation for an ERB meeting, specifications describing new aspects of HTML were made electronically available for ERB members to read. Then, at the meeting itself, the proponent explained some of the rationale behind the specification, and then dearly hoped that all who were present also concurred that the encapsulated ideas were sound. Questions such as, `should a particular feature be included, or should we kick it out,' would be considered. Each representative would air his point of view. If all went well, the specification might eventually see daylight and become a standard. At the time of writing, the next HTML standard, code-named *Cougar*, has begun its long journey in this direction.

The BLINK tag was ousted in an HTML ERB meeting. Netscape would only abolish it if Microsoft agreed to get rid of MARQUEE; the deal was struck and both tags disappeared. Both of these extensions have always been considered slightly goofy by all parties. Many tough decisions were to be made about the OBJECT specification. Out of a chaos of several different tags - EMBED, APP, APPLET, DYNSRC and so on - all associated with embedding different types of information in HTML documents, a single OBJECT tag was chosen in April, 1996. This OBJECT tag becomes part of the HTML standard, but not until 1997.

April 1996: The W3 Consortium working draft on Scripting comes out

Based on an initial draft by Charlie Kindel, and, in turn, derived from Netscape's extensions for JavaScript, a W3C working draft on the subject of Scripting was written by Dave Raggett. In one form or another, this draft should eventually become part of standard HTML.

July 1996: Microsoft seems more interested than first imagined in open standards

In April 1996, Microsoft's Internet Explorer became available for Macintosh and Windows 3.1 systems.

Thomas Reardon had been excited by the Web even at the second WWW conference held in Darmstadt, Germany in 1995. One year later, he seemed very interested in the standardization process and apparently wanted Microsoft to do things the right way with the W3C and with the IETF. Traditionally, developers are somewhat disparaging about Microsoft, so this was an interesting turn of events. It should be said that Microsoft did, of course, invent tags of their own, just as did

Netscape. These included the remarkable MARQUEE tag that caused great mirth among the more academic HTML community. The MARQUEE tag made text dance about all over the screen - not exactly a feature you would expect from a serious language concerned with structural mark-up such as paragraphs, headings and lists.

The worry that a massive introduction of proprietary products would kill the Web continued. Netscape acknowledged that vendors needed to push ahead of the standards process and innovate. They pointed out that, if users like a particular Netscape innovation, then the market would drive it to become a de facto standard. This seemed quite true at the time and, indeed, Netscape has innovated on top of that standard again. It's precisely this sequence of events that Dave Raggett and the World Wide Web Consortium were trying to avoid.

December 1996: Work on `Cougar' is begun

The HTML ERB became the HTML Working Group and began to work on `Cougar', the next version of HTML with completion late Spring, 1997, eventually to become HTML 4. With all sorts of innovations for the disabled and support for international languages, as well as providing style sheet support, extensions to forms, scripting and much more, HTML 4 breaks away from the simplicity and charm of HTML of earlier years!

Dave Raggett, co-editor of the HTML 4 specification, at work composing at the keyboard at his home in Boston.

January 1997: HTML 3.2 is ready

Success! In January 1997, the W3 Consortium formally endorsed HTML 3.2 as an HTML cross-industry specification. HTML 3.2 had been reviewed by all member organizations, including major browser vendors such as Netscape and Microsoft. This meant that the specification was now stable and approved of by most Web players. By providing a neutral forum, the W3 Consortium had successfully obtained agreement upon a standard version of HTML. There was great rejoicing, indeed. HTML 3.2 took the existing IETF HTML 2 standard and incorporated features from HTML+ and HTML 3. HTML 3.2 included tables, applets, text flow around images, subscripts and superscripts.

One might well ask why HTML 3.2 was called HTML 3.2 and not, let's say, HTML 3.1 or HTML 3.5. The version number is open to discussion just as much as is any other aspect of HTML. The version number is often one of the last details to be decided.

Key TakeAways -----

- HTML was first designed as a science project at CERN by Tim Berners-Lee

- This markup language was the single greatest contributor to the rapid expansion of the Internet during the 1990s

- Modern HTML is a flexible language that powers advanced semantic elements, responsiveness, and rich multimedia content

W3C VS. WHATWG -----

The W3C used to manage the evolution of web protocols, but the monopoly ended in 2004 when a group of highly influential stakeholders established the Web Hypertext Application Technology Working Group (WHATWG).

Members of WHATWG stated that they "were becoming increasingly concerned about the W3C's direction with XHTML and its lack of interest in HTML." They took a more pragmatic approach to satisfy the needs of browser vendors in real time without waiting for a lengthy standardization process.

The struggle between the two organizations was full of ups and downs, but WHATWG eventually prevailed. They convinced the W3C to return to the standardization of traditional HTML and recommend the then new version called HTML 5.

This practically turned WHATWG into the leading authority in the field, so it officially became the sole moderator of contemporary markup protocols in 2019. Their HTML 5 version is still active, but most developers know it by the name HTML Living Standard.

WHAT NEXT FOR HTML? -----

Now that HTML is in the living standard mode we shouldn't expect huge leaps in the future. On the contrary, this markup language will likely see lots of small improvements that will further enhance its functionality. Most importantly, all of these changes will remain backward compatible to ensure the functionality of the existing sites and web infrastructures.

Famous Browsers -----

The following are some of the most popular browsers that entirely adapt to the HTML5 standards.

Browser	Company	Decription
WorldWideWeb(Nexus)	CERN	This is the first browser in the history of the internet.

Browser	Company	Decription
		Tim Berners Lee developed it as an open-source project to assist the scientists at Cern laboratories and discontinued it in 1994.
Internet Explorer	Microsoft Inc	Microsoft created this graphical interfaced browser in 1995. It has a series of browsers and is incorporated into the Windows operating system as the default browser. Moreover, it has the latest form as **Microsoft Edge**.
Google Chrome	Google Inc	This is the most popular browser that came into existence in 2008. Google Chrome has a huge community of users. Also, its popularity is due to its fast speed, sleek interface, countless extensions, add-ons, and malware filtering.

Browser	Company	Decription
Mozilla Firefox	Mozilla Foundation	This foundation developed it as Firefox later named Mozilla Firefox. Mozilla Firefox has various features that give flexibility to the user to perform various tasks. Also, it gives a huge add-on platform to assist the users. Further, the browser also provides malware filtering. It is also one of the most popular browsers today.
Opera	Opera Softwares	It was originally developed by Telenor as a research assistant in 1994. It is one of the top browsers and most popular on mobiles due to its speed and performance.
Safari	Apple Inc	The users of the iPhone and Mac get in touch mostly with the safari browser. It has fast speed and the best content delivery system. Apple

Browser	Company	Decription
		developed it in 2003.
UC Browser	Alibaba Group	As of 2018, the UC browser is the most popular mobile browser. Developed in 2004 and covered a large marketplace speedily. It provides the best performance for mobile users. It is best known for its speed and usability.

Important Tags -----

<!Doctype>	It tells the browser about the version of HTML

<html>	<html> is the opening tag of any HTML document. It is the parent element of all the markup.
<head>	This **element** contains meta-data about the document. Meta-data is the information of the document information. e.g title, subject, location, etc
<title>	The title of the document is defined by this element.
</title>	It is the closing tag of the title element.
</head>	</head> is the closing tag of head element.
<body>	The body element, all visible content is contained in this element.
<h2>	It is the heading of the document. It is the second most bigger heading.
</h2>	The closing tag of the h2 heading.

<p>	The paragraph element defines paragraphs in a document.
</p>	The closing tag of paragraph.
</body>	Closing tag of body element.
</html>	And finally, the /html tag tells the end of the document.

Widely Used Tags -----

Element	Description
<p>	The paragraph element is required on almost every web page.
<h1>...<h6>	HTML headings are also very important to divide the text into different sub-sections into web pages.

Element	Description
<a>	To include hyperlinks, this tag is very useful and hence widely used on web pages.
<img>	We insert images in documents by employing this singleton HTML5 element.
<link>	This is another tag from the family of empty HTML elements to include external stylesheets in our document.
<script>	We include an external script by employing this HTML5 element.
<ul>	This element is utilized to insert an unordered list in a document.
<ol>	To include ordered HTML list, we use this element.
<table>	To organize tabular data, we can create tables with the help of this element.

Element	Description
<form>	This element is helpful to define forms and hold different input fields.

All About HTML -----

HTML Essentials: From Beginner to Pro

Introduction

HTML, or HyperText Markup Language, is the backbone of the web, serving as the standard language for creating web pages and applications. It's a markup language that uses a system of tags to structure and display content on the internet. Understanding HTML is fundamental for anyone looking to delve into web development, as it provides the foundation upon which all websites are built. This guide is designed to take you from the basics to advanced techniques, equipping you with the knowledge to create professional, well-structured web pages.

What is HTML?

HTML is a markup language, which means it is designed to describe the structure of web pages using a series of elements represented by tags. Each tag provides a specific function, such as defining a paragraph, a heading, an image, or a link. HTML elements are the building blocks of web pages, allowing developers to create complex layouts and interactive features.

Getting Started with HTML

To start coding in HTML, you'll need a text editor and a web browser. Text editors like Visual Studio Code, Sublime Text, or even Notepad++ provide a user-friendly environment for writing HTML. Once you have your text editor set up, you can create your first HTML document by saving a file with the .html extension.

Here's a basic example of an HTML document:

```
<html>

<!DOCTYPE html>

<html>

<head>

   <title>My First Web Page</title>

</head>

<body>

   <h1>Welcome to My Website</h1>

   <p>This is my first web page created using HTML.</p>

</body>

</html>
```

This code defines a simple web page with a title, a heading, and a paragraph. The `<!DOCTYPE html>` declaration specifies that the document is an HTML5 document.

Basic HTML Structure

An HTML document is divided into two main parts: the head and the body. The `<head>` element contains meta-information about the document, such as its title and links to stylesheets. The `<body>` element contains the actual content of the web page, including text, images, and links.

- *Headings and Paragraphs*: HTML provides six levels of headings, from `<h1>` to `<h6>`, with `<h1>` being the highest level. Paragraphs are defined using the `<p>` tag.

- Links and Navigation : Links are created using the `<a>` tag with the `href` attribute specifying the URL. Navigation menus can be built by combining multiple links.

Text Formatting

HTML offers various tags for formatting text, such as `<b>` for bold, `<i>` for italics, and `<u>` for underlining. Lists are another important element, with ordered lists created using `<ol>` and unordered lists using `<ul>`, and list items defined by `<li>`.

Working with Images

Images can be added to web pages using the `<img>` tag, with the `src` attribute specifying the image source and the `alt` attribute providing alternative text for accessibility. For example:

<img src="image.jpg" alt="A beautiful scenery">

Tables

Tables are used to display data in a tabular format, with the `<table>` tag defining the table, `<tr>` defining table rows, `<th>` defining table headers, and

`<td>` defining table cells. Tables can be styled using CSS to improve their appearance.

Forms and Input

Forms are crucial for collecting user input on websites. The `<form>` tag is used to create a form, and it contains various input elements such as text fields (`<input type="text">`), checkboxes (`<input type="checkbox">`), radio buttons (`<input type="radio">`), and submit buttons (`<input type="submit">`). Properly structured forms ensure efficient data collection and user interaction.

Semantic HTML

Semantic HTML involves using HTML5 elements that clearly describe their meaning, improving accessibility and SEO. Examples include `<article>`, `<section>`, `<nav>`, and `<footer>`. These elements make it easier for search engines and screen readers to understand the structure and content of a web page.

Advanced HTML Features

HTML5 introduces new features such as audio (`<audio>`) and video (`<video>`) elements, the `<canvas>` element for drawing graphics, and support for Scalable Vector Graphics (SVG). These features allow for richer multimedia and interactive content without relying on external plugins.

Best Practices and SEO

Writing clean, readable HTML code is crucial for maintainability and SEO. This includes using proper indentation, comments, and meaningful tag names. Additionally, optimizing HTML for search engines involves using appropriate meta tags, headings, and alt text for images.

Conclusion

HTML is the foundation of web development. By mastering HTML, you'll be well-equipped to create structured, accessible, and visually appealing web pages. This guide provides a comprehensive overview of HTML, from the basics to advanced features, ensuring you have the knowledge and skills to succeed in web development.

Last But Not Least -----

HTML Essentials: From Beginner to Pro

Table of Contents

---

1. Introduction

HTML, or HyperText Markup Language, is the backbone of the web, serving as the standard language for creating web pages and applications. It's a markup language that uses a system of tags to structure and display content on the internet. Understanding HTML is fundamental for anyone looking to delve into web development, as it provides the foundation upon which all websites are built. This guide is designed to take you from the basics to advanced techniques, equipping you with the knowledge to create professional, well-structured web pages.

2. Understanding HTML

What is HTML?

HTML is a markup language, which means it is designed to describe the structure of web pages using a series of elements represented by tags. Each tag provides a specific function, such as defining a paragraph, a heading, an image, or a link. HTML elements are the building blocks of web pages, allowing developers to create complex layouts and interactive features.

History of HTML

HTML was created by Tim Berners-Lee in 1991. It has evolved through various versions, with HTML5 being the latest standard. HTML5 introduced many new features that make it easier to build rich, interactive websites.

Importance of HTML in Web Development

HTML is essential because it is the standard markup language used to create web pages. It ensures that web content is structured correctly and can be displayed consistently across different browsers and devices. Without HTML, the web as we know it would not exist.

3. Getting Started with HTML

Choosing a Text Editor

There are many text editors available for writing HTML, including:

- **Visual Studio Code** : A powerful, open-source code editor with many extensions.

- **Sublime Text** : A lightweight, fast editor with a clean interface.

- **Notepad++** : A free source code editor that supports multiple programming languages.

Installing Web Browsers

To view and test your HTML pages, you need a web browser. Popular options include:

- Google Chrome

- Mozilla Firefox

- Safari

Setting Up a Local Server (Optional)

While not strictly necessary for HTML development, setting up a local server can be beneficial for testing more complex web applications. Tools like XAMPP or WAMP make it easy to set up a local server environment on your computer.

4. Basic HTML Structure

Introduction to HTML Tags

HTML tags are the building blocks of HTML. They define elements within a web page. Tags are enclosed in angle brackets, and most have an opening and closing tag.

Example:

```html
```

```
<p>This is a paragraph.</p>
```

Anatomy of an HTML Document

An HTML document has a standard structure that includes a `<!DOCTYPE html>` declaration, and `<html>`, `<head>`, and `<body>` tags.

Example:
```html
<!DOCTYPE html>
<html>
<head>
    <title>My First Web Page</title>
</head>
<body>
    <h1>Welcome to My Website</h1>
    <p>This is my first web page created using HTML.</p>
</body>
</html>
```

Creating Your First HTML Document

Follow these steps to create your first HTML document:

1. Open your text editor.

2. Type the basic HTML structure.

3. Save the file with a `.html` extension.

4. Open the file in your web browser to see your first web page.

5. Text Formatting

Headings and Paragraphs

Headings are used to define the headings of sections on a web page, with `<h1>` being the highest level and `<h6>` the lowest. Paragraphs are defined with the `<p>` tag.

Example:
```html
<h1>Main Heading</h1>

<h2>Subheading</h2>

<p>This is a paragraph of text.</p>
```

Text Formatting Tags (Bold, Italics, Underline)

HTML provides tags to format text. Some of the most common ones include:

- `<b>` for bold text

- `<i>` for italic text

- `<u>` for underlined text

Example:

```html
<p>This is <b>bold</b> text.</p>

<p>This is <i>italic</i> text.</p>

<p>This is <u>underlined</u> text.</p>
```


Lists (Ordered and Unordered)

Lists are used to group related items. Ordered lists (`<ol>`) use numbers, while unordered lists (`<ul>`) use bullets.

Example:

```html
<ol>
    <li>First item</li>

    <li>Second item</li>

    <li>Third item</li>
</ol>


<ul>
```

```
  <li>First item</li>
  <li>Second item</li>
  <li>Third item</li>
</ul>
```

6. Links and Navigation

Creating Hyperlinks

Hyperlinks are created using the `<a>` tag with the `href` attribute.

Example:
```html
<a href="https://www.example.com">Visit Example.com</a>
```

Linking to External Websites

To link to an external website, use the full URL in the `href` attribute.

Example:
```html
```

```
<a href="https://www.google.com" target="_blank">Open Google in a new tab</a>
```

Navigation Bars and Menus

Navigation bars help users navigate your website. They can be created using lists and styled with CSS.

Example:
```html
<nav>
  <ul>
    <li><a href="#home">Home</a></li>
    <li><a href="#about">About</a></li>
    <li><a href="#contact">Contact</a></li>
  </ul>
</nav>
```

7. Working with Images

Inserting Images

Images are added using the `<img>` tag, which requires the `src` attribute to specify the image source.

Example:
```html
<img src="image.jpg" alt="A beautiful scenery">
```

Image Attributes (Alt Text, Width, Height)

The `alt` attribute provides alternative text for images, which is important for accessibility. You can also set the width and height of an image.

Example:
```html
<img src="image.jpg" alt="A beautiful scenery" width="500" height="300">
```

Image Formats and Optimization

Common image formats include JPEG, PNG, and GIF. JPEG is best for photographs, PNG for images requiring transparency, and GIF for animations. Optimize images to reduce file size and improve page load times.

8. Tables

Creating Tables

Tables are created using the `<table>` tag. Rows are defined with `<tr>`, headers with `<th>`, and data cells with `<td>`.

Example:
```html
<table>
  <tr>
    <th>Header 1</th>
    <th>Header 2</th>
  </tr>
  <tr>
    <td>Data 1</td>
    <td>Data 2</td>
  </tr>
</table>
```

Table Headers, Rows, and Columns

Table headers provide context for the data in each column, making it easier to understand.

Styling Tables with CSS

You can style tables with CSS to improve their appearance. For example, you can add borders, padding, and background colors.

Example:

```html
<style>
  table, th, td {
    border: 1px solid black;
    border-collapse: collapse;
  }
  th, td {
    padding: 10px;
  }
  th {
    background-color: #f2f2f2;
  }
</style>
```

9. Forms and Input

Building Forms

Forms are used to collect user input. They are created using the `<form>` tag and various input elements.

Example:

```html
<form action="/submit" method="post">
    <label for="name">Name:</label>
    <input type="text" id="name" name="name"><br><br>
    <label for="email">Email:</label>
    <input type="email" id="email" name="email"><br><br>
    <input type="submit" value="Submit">
</form>
```


Form Elements and Attributes

Forms can include text fields, checkboxes, radio buttons, and more. Each input element has attributes such as `type`, `name`, and `value`.

Form Validation and Submission

Forms can be validated on the client side using HTML attributes like `required` and `pattern`, or on the server side using scripts.

Example:

```html
<form action="/submit" method="post">

  <label for="email">Email:</label>

  <input type="email" id="email" name="email" required><br><br>

  <input type="submit" value="Submit">

</form>
```

10. Semantic HTML

Understanding Semantic Elements

Semantic HTML uses tags that describe the meaning of the content. This makes the code more readable and accessible.

Semantic Tags for Content Structure

Common semantic tags include `<header>`, `<nav>`,

`<main>`, `<article>`, `<section>`, `<aside>`, and `<footer>`.

Example:

```html
```

```
<header>
  <h1>Website Title</h1>
  <nav>
    <ul>
      <li><a href="#home">Home</a></li>
      <li><a href="#about">About</a></li>
      <li><a href="#contact">Contact</a></li>
    </ul>
  </nav>
</header>
<main>
  <article>
    <h2>Article Title</h2>
    <p>Article content goes here.</p>
  </article>
  <aside>
    <h3>Related Content</h3>
    <p>Links to related content go here.</p>
  </aside>
</main>
<footer>
  <p>Footer content goes here.</p>
</footer>
```

Benefits of Semantic HTML

Semantic HTML improves accessibility, SEO, and maintainability by providing clear structure and meaning to web content.

11. Advanced HTML Features

HTML5 Elements

HTML5 introduced new elements for multimedia, graphics, and better structure.

Audio and Video Elements

The `<audio>` and `<video>` tags allow you to embed multimedia content directly into web pages.

Example:
```html
<audio controls>
  <source src="audio.mp3" type="audio/mpeg">
  Your browser does not support the audio element.
</audio>

<video controls width="500">
```

```
  <source src="video.mp4" type="video/mp4">

  Your browser does not support the video tag.

</video>
```

Canvas and SVG for Graphics

The `<canvas>` element is used for drawing graphics on the fly, while SVG (Scalable Vector Graphics) is used for defining vector-based graphics.

Example:
```html
<canvas id="myCanvas" width="200" height="100" style="border:1px solid #000000;"></canvas>

<script>
   var c = document.getElementById("myCanvas");

   var ctx = c.getContext("2d");

   ctx.moveTo(0,0);

   ctx.lineTo(200,100);

   ctx.stroke();
</script>
```

Geolocation and Local Storage

HTML5 APIs allow access to device features like geolocation and local storage, enabling more interactive and personalized web experiences.

Example:

```html
<script>
  if (navigator.geolocation) {
    navigator.geolocation.getCurrentPosition(showPosition);
  } else {
    alert("Geolocation is not supported by this browser.");
  }

  function showPosition(position) {
    alert("Latitude: " + position.coords.latitude +
    "\nLongitude: " + position.coords.longitude);
  }
</script>
```

12. Best Practices and SEO

Writing Clean and Readable HTML

Maintain a consistent coding style with proper indentation and comments to make your code readable and maintainable.

SEO Optimization

Use appropriate meta tags, headings, and alt text for images to optimize your HTML for search engines.

Example:

```
<html>

<meta name="description" content="A brief description of the web page.">

<meta name="keywords" content="HTML, web development, coding">

</html>
```

Accessibility

Ensure your web pages are accessible to all users by using semantic HTML, providing alternative text for images, and following best practices for keyboard navigation and screen readers.

Example:

```html
<img src="image.jpg" alt="Description of the image">
```

13. Conclusion and Next Steps

Congratulations on completing this guide! You now have a solid foundation in HTML and are well on your way to becoming a proficient web developer. The next steps involve learning CSS for styling and JavaScript for interactivity, which will enable you to build more complex and dynamic websites.

14. Appendix: HTML Cheat Sheet

- **Basic Tags** : `<!DOCTYPE html>`, `<html>`, `<head>`, `<title>`, `<body>`, `<h1>` to `<h6>`, `<p>`, `<a>`, `<img>`, `<ul>`, `<ol>`, `<li>`

- **Form Tags** : `<form>`, `<input>`, `<label>`, `<button>`, `<select>`, `<textarea>`

- **Table Tags** : `<table>`, `<tr>`, `<th>`, `<td>`

- **Semantic Tags** : `<header>`, `<nav>`, `<main>`, `<article>`, `<section>`, `<aside>`, `<footer>`

- **Multimedia Tags** : `<audio>`, `<video>`, `<canvas>`, `<svg>`

15. Glossary

- **HTML** : HyperText Markup Language, the standard language for creating web pages.

- **CSS** : Cascading Style Sheets, a language used to describe the presentation of a document written in HTML.

- **JavaScript** : A programming language used to create dynamic and interactive effects on web pages.

-   **SEO**   : Search Engine Optimization, the practice of optimizing web pages to rank higher in search engine results.

-   **Accessibility**   : The practice of making web content usable for people of all abilities and disabilities.

Images -----

HTML

Hyper Text Markup Language

```
document.getElementById(div).innerHTML

else if (i==2)

{

    var atpos=inputs[i].indexOf('@');
    var dotpos=inputs[i].lastIndexOf(':');
    if (atpos<1 || dotpos<atpos+2
        document.getElementById('errEmail');

    else
        document.getElementById(div).innerHTML

}
    ice if (i==5)
```